anythink

STICKMEN'S GUIDE TO MOUNTAINS AND VALLEYS
IN LAYERS

Thanks to the creative team:
Senior Editor: Alice Peebles
Fact checking: Kate Mitchell
Design: www.collaborate.agency

Original edition copyright 2016 by Hungry Tomato Ltd.

Hungry Tomato™
A division of Lerner Publishing Group, Inc.
241 First Avenue North
Minneapolis, MN 55401 USA

For reading levels and more information, look up this title at
www.lernerbooks.com.

Main body text set in Avenir Next Medium 9.5/12. Typeface provided by
Linotype AG.

Library of Congress Cataloging-in-Publication Data

The Cataloging-in-Publication Data for *Stickmen's Guide to Mountains and
Valleys in Layers* is on file at the Library of Congress.
ISBN 978-1-5124-0618-4 (lib. bdg.)
ISBN 978-1-5124-1179-9 (pbk.)
ISBN 978-1-5124-0932-1 (EB pdf)

Manufactured in the United States of America
1 - VP - 7/15/16

STICKMEN'S GUIDE TO MOUNTAINS AND VALLEYS

IN LAYERS

by Catherine Chambers

Illustrated by John Paul de Quay

HUNGRY TOMATO.

Contents

Mountains and Valleys

Earth, the Sun, and other planets in our solar system formed nearly 4.6 billion years ago. Gases and dust in space collided, forming clumps that enlarged as their gravity attracted more material. On the clump that became Earth, a cooling crust cracked into huge pieces called tectonic plates, which cover hotter layers and a hardened core.

Mountaintops

Where winters are very cold, snow and ice reach far down the mountains. In warm parts of the world, snow and ice give way to alpine trees and plants.

Plains

Down on the plains, vast grasslands stretch out in both cool and hot climates. Here, wild animals roam, and farmers herd cattle and grow grains.

Under the Crust

Below the plains, rivers cut deep down into the rock. Even deeper, Earth shakes and hot volcanic magma pushes up through the crust.

Earth's Core

At the center of Earth, a soft, searing hot outer core wraps around the hard inner core. Both parts of the core are made mostly of metal.

Snow Power

Many great rivers would not flow without snowy mountaintops. High in central Asia's Himalaya range, trickling waters from snowmelt and icy meltwater caves feed the mighty River Ganges below. Glaciers' dripping bases run into many other rivers. This glacial meltwater, rushing down steep slopes at speed, is perfect for turning turbines to create electricity. This is Hydroelectric Power (HEP) and it provides almost 65 percent of all electricity in the mountainous country of Austria.

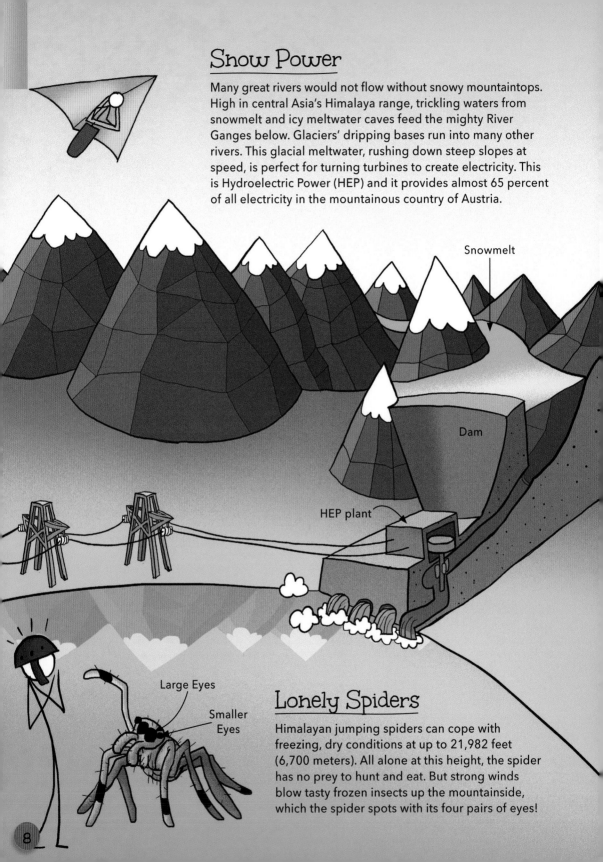

Snowmelt

Dam

HEP plant

Large Eyes

Smaller Eyes

Lonely Spiders

Himalayan jumping spiders can cope with freezing, dry conditions at up to 21,982 feet (6,700 meters). All alone at this height, the spider has no prey to hunt and eat. But strong winds blow tasty frozen insects up the mountainside, which the spider spots with its four pairs of eyes!

Snowy Peaks

We live on the top crusty layer of Earth—the solid, brittle lithosphere. Here, the hardest rocks wear down more slowly than the softer rocks, leaving high, windy mountain peaks coated with snow and thick ice.

Challenge at the Top

Mount Everest is the world's highest peak above sea level, rising to 29,035 feet (8,850 m). It's a magnet for serious mountaineers. In freezing conditions, they use spiked crampons on their shoes to cling to the ice, and an ice pick to pull themselves up.

Helmet

Carabiner
(safety rope hook)

Ice Pick

Crampons

Ridge

Glacier
(Ice Tongue)

Clinging On

Clusters of spongy, plant-like lichens cling to the rocks on the lowest, warmer parts of this layer. Lichens are combinations of fungi and algae.

Tough Alpine Life

Down the mountain, the tree line marks the alpine layer. Here, trees' waxy, needle-like leaves stop them from freezing or drying out in winter. Creatures such as small shrews hibernate in winter. Their heart rate slows down so they use little energy.

Glacier

Alpine Sports

Tree Line

Corrie Lake

Long Tail

Wide Feet
(for walking in snow)

Extreme Survivor

The thick-furred snow leopard lives on central Asia's craggy mountain ranges, at up to 17,000 feet (5,000 m). It hunts blue mountain sheep and ibex.

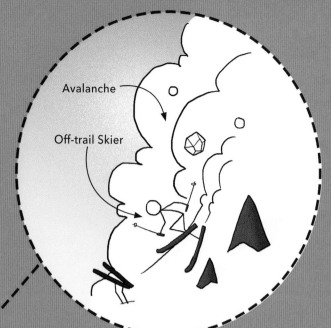

Avalanche

Off-trail Skier

Spectacular Sports

In the United States, nearly 10 million people ski or snowboard each year. Most glide down trails of specially prepared, hard-packed snow. But more daring, off-trail sports take place in higher backcountry. Here, skiers powder-ski fast between trees on loose, unstable snow. Cat skiers, named after the snowcats that transport them, descend down deep, steep trails. Splitboarders climb high on skis, then clip the skis together to board their way down again. These thrill-seekers carry GPS devices to beam their position if avalanches of snow bury them.

Icy Lakes

Rounded lakes called corries form on mountainsides. They begin in small hollows, where snow layers pack down hard and ice is created. Gravity pulls the ice downward in a circular motion, abrading, or scouring out, a bigger hole that fills with water. Many corrie lakes formed thousands of years ago.

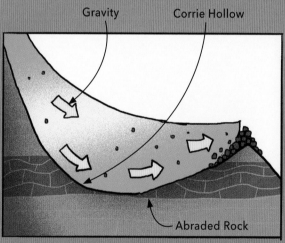

Gravity

Corrie Hollow

Abraded Rock

Alpine Diapensia Plant

Tight and Low Mound

Dark Leaves

Brave Flowers

Low-growing, cushion-shaped plants hug the rocks to resist high alpine winds. Many have long taproots to anchor them. Their tightly packed flowers bloom quickly in the short summers that last three months or so. Dark leaves absorb the sunlight that they use to make the plant's food.

Forested Slopes

Lower, gentler mountain slopes are known as the montane layer, and they have thicker soil where vast forests of trees, bushes, and grasses grow. Close to the hot equator, tropical and subtropical trees flourish. Nearer the chilly poles, hardy evergreen spruces and pines survive.

Cool Coffee

Coffee grown on bushes high up has the best flavor. Wild coffee comes from the mountains of Ethiopia in East Africa and has been cultivated for more than six hundred years.

Red Coffee Berries

Coffee Bean Inside

Mountain Slopes

Coffee Farm

Orchard

Widening River

Pine and Spruce Trees

Bright Birds

Subtropical montane forest birds are often brightly colored to attract a mate among the trees' shadows. The vivid Green-tailed Sunbird occupies a broad range, from the forests of western Nepal and northern India down into Southeast Asia. The Golden-browed Chlorophonia lives in the canopy of the highland forests of southern Central America.

Green-tailed Sunbird

Golden-browed Chlorophonia

Juniper and Conifer Forest

Montane Apple Orchard

Sedges

Montane Mammals

Both hot and cold montane climates are rich habitats for mammals, both large and small. In North America, the black bear climbs forest trees to reach berries and fruit, but also eats roots, fish, and insects. The black bear actually comes in a variety of colors, but all have thick fur to help them stay warm during their winter hibernation. In eastern Africa, furry mountain gorillas live in high cloud forests. They feed on forest fruits, bamboo shoots, thistles, and dried grasses.

Skeleton Trees

These dried-out bent spruce or pine trees are called *krummholz*, which means "twisted timber." Krummholz are stunted by extreme winter cold and blown in one direction by severe freezing winds. As they bend, branches touch the ground. Roots can grow down from these branches, anchoring the tree firmly to the ground.

Wind Direction ⟶

On the Plains

Vast grasslands spread out beneath mountain foothills, sometimes on raised plateaus. North America's prairies, South America's pampas, central Asia's cool steppes, and Africa's hot savannah have provided highways for migrating peoples and creatures.

Riches Beneath

Mining and oil and gas extraction break up the grasslands' wild beauty. The flat plains make it easier to transport minerals and energy sources than hilly terrain.

Wheat Prairie

Combine-harvester

Oil and Gas Extraction

Prairie Horses

Grassland

Cattle Herder

Farming on the Plains

Many grasslands have been cleared to cultivate grass species such as wheat and corn. In Africa, these are planted together with beans, which help fertilize the soil. Argentina has recently converted some pampas to huge vineyards, though cattle are still herded on these vast grasslands.

Wheat Field

Attwater's Prairie Chicken

Prairie Grasses and Flowers

Hiding in the Grass

Carpets of grasses and flowers are perfect camouflage for small mammals and birds. The mottled brown Attwater's Prairie Chicken hides among Texas coast prairie bluestem and switchgrass plants. But the adult male pops up in shorter grasses to call for a mate. His loud boom reaches a half-mile (800 m).

Teeming with Life

Grassland plains are teeming with wildlife. Africa's savannah creatures range from tiny termites to huge elephants, Earth's largest land animal. Termites build dirt mounds that can reach 17 feet (5 m). The termites' constant burrowing helps to circulate nutrients, keeping the soil healthy. Large grassland mammals, such as buffalo and antelope, fertilize the soil with their droppings, which contain seeds that are then scattered across the vast grassland.

Termite Mound

The Valley Floor

Glaciers carve broad valleys down through mountains. Rivers cut deep natural highways into the lowlands, widening as they reach the sea. Manmade transport systems take advantage of the shallow slopes far along a river's course.

Ice Valleys

Glaciers begin as compacted snow that changes into ice made of large, dense crystals. This heavy ice gathers into a tongue that scrapes a broad, deep U-shaped valley into the rock beneath. Sometimes glaciers reshape the base of river valleys by sheer power. Down at the bottom, the glacier dumps piles of eroded rocks that it carries along. Tourists visit active glaciers at their base, such as the Perito Moreno Glacier in Argentina, which is 19 miles (30 kilometers) long.

Glacier Tongue

Moraine Rocks and Sediment

Wide, Navigable River at the Base of the Valley

Reeds

Seed Head

Bulrushes

River Power

Rivers carve steep, narrow, V-shaped valleys until they reach low, flat land. Here, they weaken, widen, and wind, no longer able to cut downwards. Meeting the sea, rivers may split into tiny rivulets, spreading out into a delta. India's River Ganges has the world's largest delta, with an area of 38,610 square miles (100,000 square kilometers).

Big Fish

Wide rivers teem with large fish. One of these is the salmon, which lays its eggs in river gravel beds in autumn. In spring, the fish hatch. After a few years in the river they swim far out to sea. Here, they feed on sand eels and herring until they return to the river once more.

Shipping for Transporting Goods

Railroad track along Level River Valley Bottom

Rushes and Reeds

Grass-like reeds and rushes grow near the banks of a river, low down on its course. Bulrushes are habitats for fish and amphibians such as frogs and newts. Bulrush leaves and spikes are edible.

Reed Habitat for Fish and Amphibians

Deep in the Canyon

Canyons are plunging, steep-sided valleys. Some are cut by thin rivers, while others are splits caused by the movement of tectonic plates deep in Earth's crust. The deepest canyon is Tibet's Yarlung Zangbo Canyon, at 17,490 feet (5,300 m).

Ancient Canyon Dwellers

Many prehistoric humans lived in canyon caves. They used rock pigments to depict their lives on the walls. East Africa's Olduvai Gorge holds some of the oldest fossilized human remains.

Ancient Rock Art

Rock Layers

River, Restricted by Canyon Sides

Buzzing with Birds

Canyons are remote havens for some of the world's rarest birds. Great eagles, condors, and falcons circle up above, their sharp eyes focusing on prey far below. High, dry ledges are perfect for their nests. Lower down, small, bright perching birds, such as warblers, flycatchers, and orioles, thrive in the damp habitat.

Bubbling Waters

Hot volcanic activity lies close to the surface of some canyon floors. Here, hot magma below heats groundwater above, thrusting it up into hot waterspouts, or geysers. Boiling springs, bubbling mud pools, and steaming sprays of water are dotted across these canyons' landscapes. California's Yellowstone Park has about five hundred hot springs and geysers. Across the world in Africa's Great Rift Valley, people in Kenya use volcanic steam wells to harness geothermal energy (heat energy made inside Earth).

Bald Eagle

Hot Spring

Spouting Geyser

Steam Vent

Heated Groundwater   Volcanic Magma

Slithering Along

The rocky habitats of canyons are perfect for snakes, while lizards are also at home by the river. In the Grand Canyon there are forty-seven species of reptiles. Here, great gila monster lizards thrive among the wispy tamarisk bushes. Long ago in the canyons' sandstone rocks, dinosaurs left their footprints.

Lizard

Rattlesnake

19

Down the Mine

Deep in Earth's crust, humans drill down for precious minerals and metals embedded in rock. Most hard minerals formed from hot volcanic magma. Slow cooling and high pressure caused some magma particles to crystallize into sparkling stones.

Precious Metals

Gold is a metallic element that can be found in river deposits. But most is embedded in veins of quartz rock, deep below Earth's surface.

Gold Deposit

Coal or Ore Transported to the Surface for Processing

Brilliant Diamonds

Diamond mines are built as terraced craters so large that they can be seen from space. Diamonds are hard, heat-resistant carbons. They began to form more than 4 billion years ago in the Earth's hot mantle, and were thrust up by deep volcanic eruptions. Russia has over half the world's largest diamond mines.

Diamond Mine Terraces

Rig

Sea Level

Deck

Piles

Sea Floor

Wells

Oil and Gas Reservoir

Crushed Creatures

We dig deeper for oil and gas deposits than for any other mineral. The deepest floating oil platform is Perdido, in the Gulf of Mexico. Its pipe reaches down 8,000 feet (2,450 m). Drills access pockets of fossil fuels by piercing deep layers of rock that trap them. We call them fossil fuels because they were made from tiny plants and creatures millions of years ago. Under extreme heat and pressure, they changed into oil and gas.

Shaft to Ice Pipe

Ice Slurry

Mine Hotspots

The world's deepest mine is South Africa's Mponeng gold mine, which plunges down 2.4 miles (3.87 km). It is so close to Earth's layer of hot magma that its temperature can reach more than 122°F (50°C). So ice slurry is piped down to the bottom, where it cools the air for the mine's six thousand workers.

Volcano Power

A volcano forms when Earth's crust splits apart under the force of hot, molten magma rock below. Clouds of ash and sulfurous gases shoot up from the mantle layer. Magma cools in different forms, from hard, shiny swirls of pahoehoe lava to crunchy stones.

Hot Ash Fall

Hot Rock
Tephra
"Bombs"

Gas and Ash
Column

Composite Volcano

Vent

Debris Landslide

Fumaroles (vents
where volcanic
gas escapes)

Lava Flow

Mud and Debris
Flow

Magma
Crack

Conduit

Heated
Groundwater

Magma
Chamber

Rich Volcanic Soil

In time, tephra—any material thrown up by a volcano—creates rich soils that attract farmers to the volcano's slopes. Wildflower seeds and fern spores blow across lava fields, settling in moist cracks.

Tiltmeter
Air Bubble
Vent
Electrode Sensor
Hot Magma
Moving Magma Tilting the Slope

When Will It Erupt?

Predicting the time and force of deep volcanic explosions is a challenge. Vulcanologists place tiltmeters horizontally, high on the sides of volcano vents. When hot magma rises, it pushes a bulge into a vent's surface, altering the slope. The air bubble inside the tiltmeter moves, indicating an explosion is likely to happen.

Mighty Explosions

Most recent volcanic eruptions are measured by the amount of force generated by the explosion, and the damage caused. The Tambora eruption of 1815 killed 92,000 people. With an explosive magnitude of 7 on the volcanic explosivity index (VEI), it is known as a Super-colossal eruption. Damage is not limited to human casualties. Thick ash from a volcano smothers flora and crops, killing them with heat, weight, and toxins, followed by a lack of air and light.

Most Destructive Volcanoes

1 Tambora, Indonesia, 1815
2 Santorini, Greece, 1628 BCE
3 Krakatau, Indonesia, 1883
4 Santa Maria, Guatemala, 1902
5 Mount St. Helens, United States, 1980
6 Vesuvius, Italy, 79
7 Pinatubo, Philippines, 1991
8 Mount Pelée, Martinique, 1902
9 Nevado del Ruiz, Colombia, 1985
10 Unzen, Japan, 1792

Toxic Gases
Volcanic Vent

Scaly-foot Snail

Living on Gases

Down on the ocean floor, hot toxic gases such as hydrogen sulphide shoot up through volcanic vents. Deep-sea cameras have filmed amazing life-forms surviving happily on the gases, such as the scaly-foot snail. Sharks have been spotted inside the underwater Kavachi volcano near the Solomon Islands.

Smashing Plates

Enormous cracks divide Earth's crust into a jigsaw of tectonic plates. These float on the soft asthenosphere layer, which sits at the top of the thick mantle. The plates move slowly, up to 4 inches (100 millimeters) a year, and where their boundaries meet, the crust shakes, causing earthquakes.

Tectonic Plates

North American Plate

Eurasian Plate

Arabian Plate

Caribbean Plate

Pacific Plate

Cocos Plate

African Plate

Pacific Plate

Phillippine Plate

Nazca Plate

Indian Plate

South American Plate

Indo-Australian Plate

Scotia Plate

Antarctic Plate

Radon Meter

Warning Signs

Earthquake prediction is difficult and not very successful. This hand-held meter measures changes in radon gases released as Earth's plates move. Seismometers measure Earth's tremors, while laser beams set across fault lines register movement. Changes in water table levels, stream flows, and even animal behavior are also monitored.

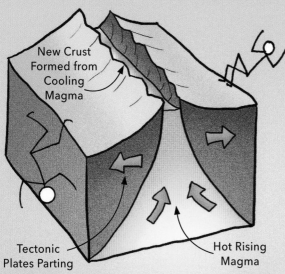

New Crust Formed from Cooling Magma

Tectonic Plates Parting

Hot Rising Magma

How Earth's Plates Move

Tectonic plates interact with each other in different ways to cause earthquakes. They might slowly collide, or slide against each other, grating as they move. Sometimes tremors are caused when the plates move apart or when one plate pushes up on top of another.

What Happens in an Earthquake?

Millions of years ago, massive movements of tectonic plates shaped Earth into the continents. Today, smaller movements can destroy buildings and entire towns and villages. Earthquakes tear cracks in roads and railroad lines, pull down bridges, and break communication links.

Measuring an Earthquake

Earthquake vibrations are measured using seismometers. Each movement is given a value of 1 to 10 on the Richter Scale. The most destructive is 10, which indicates many deaths and a lot of destruction. But tremors can affect people far from land. Some radiate into the sea, making it swell into walls of water that crash against distant shores. These devastating waves are called *tsunamis,* and they kill even more people than earthquakes.

Most Destructive Earthquakes

Place	Date	Magnitude
Off coast, Chile	1960	9.5
Alaska, USA	1964	9.2
Northern Sumatra	2004	9.1
Honshu, Japan	2011	9.0
Kamchatka, Russia	1952	9.0
Chile, off Maule coast	2010	8.8
Off coast, Ecuador	1906	8.8
Rat Island, Alaska, USA	1965	8.7
Sumatra, Indonesia	2005	8.6
Tibet and India	1950	8.6

The Center of Earth

Earth's core lies deep beneath the molten mantle and crusty lithosphere. The outer edge of the core lies nearly 1,860 miles (3,000 km) from the surface, while its center is more than 3,700 miles (6,000 km) away. The core's temperature can reach 10,832°F (6,000°C).

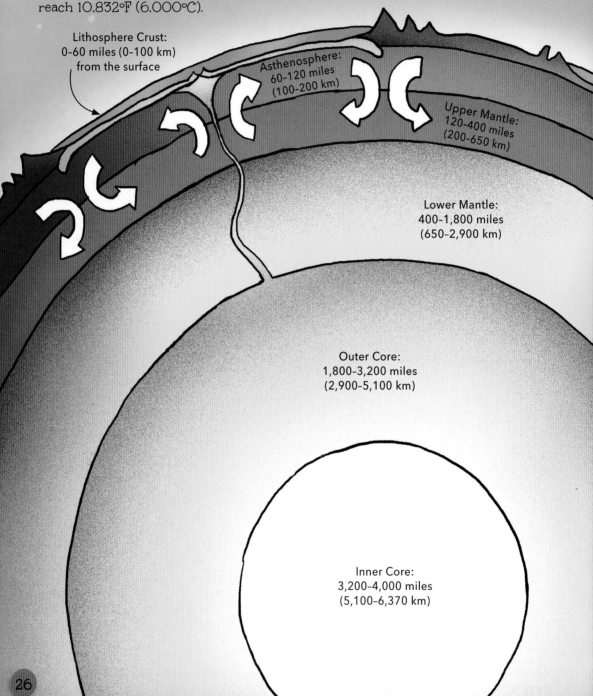

Lithosphere Crust:
0–60 miles (0–100 km)
from the surface

Asthenosphere:
60–120 miles
(100–200 km)

Upper Mantle:
120–400 miles
(200–650 km)

Lower Mantle:
400–1,800 miles
(650–2,900 km)

Outer Core:
1,800–3,200 miles
(2,900–5,100 km)

Inner Core:
3,200–4,000 miles
(5,100–6,370 km)

Earth's Magnetic Force

The planet's outer core is liquid, but the inner core mainly consists of solid iron. Billions of years ago this iron was molten, and squeezed down into the center, where it hardened. The movement of molten iron around the hard core creates an electrical current, which in turn generates Earth's magnetic field.

North Pole

Mantle

Inner Core

Magnetic Field

Convection Currents

South Pole

Earth's Crust

Hot Liquid Outer Core

Core Science

For more than one hundred years, scientists have studied the texture of Earth's core by measuring energy waves from ground tremors. First, scientists used seismometers to follow the paths of S (secondary) waves. But these could not reach Earth's solid inner core. Then, in the 1930s, scientist Inge Lehmann discovered a new P (primary) wave that could detect both of the core's layers.

Seismometer Measuring Waves from Tremor

What We Know So Far

The liquid outer core is made mostly of iron, with some nickel and oxygen gas. We do not know how hot it is because it moves up and down, varying the temperature. The hard inner core is made mostly of iron too, but may also contain nickel. At its outer edge, the inner core freezes, chilling the liquid outer core next to it. This hardens, which means that the inner core is growing at about 0.02 inches (0.5 mm) each year.

Fantastic Mountain and Valley Facts

Brave Bird

The highest nesting bird is the Himalayan Snowcock, which lives on craggy open slopes between the tree line and the snow line, at up to 15,092 feet (4,600 m). It feeds by digging with its long bill at grasses, shoots, and roots found in the rocks' cracks. The Snowcock walks up to 0.4 square miles (1 sq km) a day to find its food, as it prefers not to fly.

Super Snow Dogs

An avalanche of snow is a terrifying danger on alpine slopes. But 90 percent of people buried in an avalanche survive if they are found in the first fifteen minutes. It can take twenty people with probe poles that dig into the snow four hours to search 2.5 acres (1 hectare). But a trained rescue dog can cover the same area in thirty minutes. They can smell a human buried under 6.6 feet (2 m) of snow!

Precious Prairies

Prairies formed about eight thousand years ago and once covered 40 percent of the United States. Now, they make up just 1 percent of the land. The amazing range of prairie plants includes grasses with roots that reach 12 feet (3.6 m) down into the soil, holding the soil structure together. As the roots and flower bulbs die and break down, they enrich the soil.

The Greatest Land Mammal

The African elephant can be 11 feet (3.3 m) tall and weigh 6.6 tons (6 tonnes). It eats grasses, fruit, bark, leaves, and even whole branches of trees. The African elephant's enormous ears help to keep it cool by radiating heat from the blistering sun. Its long trunk, which helps it breathe, feed, drink, and wash, has 150,000 different muscle units!

Natural Art Gallery

More than six thousand rock engravings have been found along the deep Helankou Gorge that cuts between the Helan Mountains in China's Ningxia Region. They were created between three thousand to ten thousand years ago and include images of tigers, leopards, horses, and camels. Hunters, herders, fighters, and dancers show how humans lived so long ago.

Going for Gold

South Africa's deep Mponeng Mine (see page 21) can produce 550,000 ounces (1,560 kilograms) of gold every year. But miners have to exract 6,000 tons (5,443 tonnes) of rock each day to find that amount. At such depths, the only natural life-forms are bacteria, trapped between wet cracks. These bacteria have evolved so that they can survive without sunlight.

Terrible Tambora

In 1815, the most terrible eruption from Tambora Mountain in Indonesia (see page 23) affected the whole world. The skies grew dark with ash and sulfurous gas, smothering fields and blocking sunlight. The effects of this on weather patterns were felt for three years, bringing famine, disease, and economic depression across the globe.

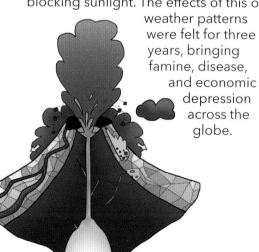

Towering Tsunami

On July 9, 1958, an earthquake along Fairweather Fault on the Alaskan coast loosened 1 billion cubic feet (30.6 million cubic meters) of rock high above Lituya Bay. Falling from 3,000 feet (914 m), the rock crashed into the water below, creating a 1,720-foot (520-m) tsunami that hit the land and swept away millions of trees.

The Future...

Scientists are always learning more about how and when Earth's geological layers formed. They are still finding out the true composition, temperature, and movement of its core. The effects of climate change on Earth's layers, and on its soils and waterways are hotly debated.

Moving Mountains

Just forty years ago, we learned how mountain ranges pushed up, folded, and crumpled when tectonic plates moved against each other. Only twenty years ago, scientists realized that mountains are still being thrust up— they are growing. So this movement must affect Earth's layers, but we have yet to find out how.

Human Footprint

Human activity is destroying delicate layers of flora and fauna. At mountain level, clearing trees for their wood or to grow crops destroys habitats that have taken thousands of years to form. Bare soil that is easily eroded is all that is left. Some climbers, walkers, and skiers trample over plants and soil. Traffic fumes in mountain valleys are polluting plant life high above.

Cost of Climate Change

Many of the lithosphere's layers are covered with soils that can be eroded easily by wind and rain. Intense storms are occurring more frequently in many parts of the world. This means that wind speeds are greater and rain more torrential, leading to faster and deeper erosion. Most scientists blame climate change for a shift in storm patterns and intensity. Earth is experiencing higher overall temperatures.

Watching Saint Elias

The Saint Elias Mountain Range, in freezing Alaska, is being closely observed. This range uplifted along the boundary between the North American and Pacific plates (see page 24). Saint Elias is really exciting for scientists as its summit is being pushed up by tectonic activity at one of the fastest rates in the world: 0.016 inches (4 mm) per year. It is also steeper than any other range, which makes its glaciers flow so fast they thin its crust. Scientists are wondering if the thinning crust will make the mountain lighter, and therefore its uplift faster. Their research continues.

Glossary

algae:
simple plant-like organisms

avalanche:
wall of tumbling snow

cloud forest:
a moist and cloudy montane tropical and subtropical evergreen forest

fungi:
spongy plant-like forms, such as a mushroom

gravity:
the force that pulls objects toward Earth and each other

ice slurry:
broken, slushy ice

lava:
hot liquid magma that has reached Earth's surface

nutrient:
food that helps living things thrive

pahoehoe:
smooth, shiny, swirling hardened lava in Hawaii

poles:
the opposite ends of Earth's axis

P wave:
primary wave from an earthquake's source, used in measuring the strength of a tremor

snowmelt:
water running off melting snow from mountains

spore:
seed-like structure of algae, fungi, and ferns

spruce:
evergreen trees with needle-like leaves

sulfurous:
containing sulfur, a hard yellow chemical element that emits a gas when burned

S wave:
secondary wave from an earthquake's source

INDEX

The Author

Catherine Chambers was born in Adelaide, South Australia, grew up in the United Kingdom and studied African History and Swahili at the School of Oriental and African Studies in London. She has written about 130 books for children and young adults, and enjoys seeking out intriguing facts for her nonfiction titles, which cover history, cultures, faiths, biography, geography, and the environment.

The Illustrator

John Paul has a BSc in Biology from the University of Sussex, United Kingdom, and a graduate certificate in animation from the University of the West of England. He devotes his spare time to growing chili peppers, perfecting his plan for a sustainable future, and caring for a small plastic dinosaur. He has three pet squid that live in the bath, which makes drawing in ink quite economical . . .

Picture Credits (abbreviations: t = top; b = bottom; c = center; l = left; r = right)
© www.shutterstock.com: 29 br.